THE ELDER
THE MOTHER TREE OF FOLKLORE

~

CHRIS HOWKINS

PUBLISHED BY
CHRIS HOWKINS

COPYRIGHT
Text and illustrations © Chris Howkins 1996

PUBLISHER
Chris Howkins, 70 Grange Road,
New Haw, ADDLESTONE, Surrey.
KT15 3RH

PRINTED
Unwin Brothers Ltd., The Gresham Press,
Old Woking, Surrey, England.
GU22 9LH

CONDITIONS OF SALE
This book is sold subject to the condition that it shall not, by way of trade or otherwise, be lent, re-sold, hired out or otherwise circulated in any form of binding or cover other than that in which it is published and without a similar condition including this condition being imposed upon the subsequent purchaser.

ALL RIGHTS RESERVED
No part of this publication may be reproduced, stored in a retrieval system, or transmitted in any form or by any means electronic, mechanical, photocopying, recording or otherwise without the prior permission of the publisher.

ISBN 0 9519348 9 9

WEATHER LORE
If it rains when Elderflowers open
It stays wet till they fade away.

CONTENTS

*
***
*

The Elder 4
Which Tree is the Elder ? 5
Hyde-Moer - The Elder Mother 6
Home Protection 6
Protecting Travellers 8
Protecting Livestock 8
Protecting Bakehouses 10
Never Cut the Elder Tree 12
Never Burn Elder Wood 14
Conflict of Faiths 17
Betrayal of Jesus 18
Elder at the Crucifixion 19
The Curse 20
Witches and Faeries 20
May Eve 22
Midsummer and St.John 23
Epiphany 24
Narcotic Visions 26
Magic Healing 28
Everyday Life 30

THE ELDER ~
THE MOTHER TREE OF FOLKLORE

Do witches really live in Elder trees? Did they really make Christ's Cross from an Elder tree? Why is it unlucky to bring Elder into the house? The folklore of the Elder is greater than for any other tree in N.W.Europe and the fascination it still holds over people today is equally impressive.

This collection of the folklore does not aim to be at all complete but is based upon those traditions that are still remembered and raised by audiences when the writer is giving talks. Therefore the raw material has come from Surrey and Sussex, north east Hampshire, east Berkshire, south west Middlesex (Spelthorne) and south Buckinghamshire but of course the people of those counties have come from far and wide, bringing with them the traditions of other districts. Thanks to them we can glimpse the world of the Mother Tree - the Elder - but it is very important to remember that it is only a glimpse and that it is not possible to recreate the full picture of this great tree.

First, a botanical note to identify the tree concerned.....

WHICH TREE IS THE ELDER ?

Botanically, the tree of this study is *Sambucus nigra* L. which is the only tree of the genus that is native to the British Isles. There is another species, *Sambucus ebulus* L., known as the Dwarf Elder or Danewort, but that is an herbaceous plant.

There are two other species of Elder tree to be found in the British countryside but these are foreign, having been able to naturalise after escaping from cultivation. These are the Red-berried Elder, *Sambucus racemosa* L. and the American Elder, *Sambucus canadensis* L.

This study deals exclusively with *Sambucus nigra,* the Common or European Elder, called the Black Elder in America to distinguish it from their own. None of these should be confused with the garden weed, *Aegopodium podagraria L.,* known as the Ground Elder, Wild Elder, Dutch Elder or Dog Eller.

HYLDE - MOER ~ THE ELDER MOTHER

Once upon a time, thousands of years ago, everything around the European peoples was believed to have its own special deity - the sun and the moon, water and fire, the animals and trees etc. One very potent tree deity was Hylde-Moer (or Hilde-vinde). She was sacred to the Elder and indeed manifested herself as the Elder tree itself.

This immediately makes the tree something special in the landscape and must therefore be treated with respect. Here then is the foundation for all the decrees or superstitions concerning what you must do, or must not do, to an Elder. She is of course a 'Good' spirit since she is a 'Mother' and like any other mother she loves those who respect her but is likely to turn on anyone who treats her badly and teach them the error of their ways. In the British Isles there is still widespread belief in the tree being protective, made clearer by the Russian belief that it is out of her love for all life that she drives away evil.

For the moment put aside any ideas that the tree is evil and associated with witches. That probably derives from the work of the Christian missionaries trying to establish the new faith. It is therefore not as old as some of the other lore and will appear later in the book.

HOME PROTECTION

The motherly protection afforded by the Elder is still well known today and many a back garden is graced by one of the trees. The owners will most probably disclaim any hint of belief in the old traditions but will, nevertheless, leave the tree well alone! Held in particularly high esteem is a self-sown Elder. After all, if the mother goddess actually chooses to come and live with you then you must be a favoured household indeed. It will not only protect the home but the plot of land as well. Where there is not one growing then it is efficacious to at least hang up a green bough over the doorway to deter evil from entering.

Home protection took the form of warding off all evil forces. These were understood to be of the spiritual kind, there being other plants valued as protection against thunderbolts, plague etc. Having said that, Elder has been regarded throughout the British Isles as a tree that deflects lightning.

Later, these ideas got transferred to the bottoms of the gardens when the outside privy was invented - one place where people wanted a sense of security. There are also two good reasons for growing Elders there. Firstly, the foliage is insect repellent and secondly the tree loves the damp rich soil which it therefore purifies as it grows. Many country cottages still have their clump of Elders at the bottom of their gardens, even if the little wooden hut has long since gone.

PROTECTING TRAVELLERS

Moving around beyond the bounds of one's sense of security was obviously hazardous. Travellers were told to carry on their person an Elder twig and then they would be safe from muggers wherever they went, (a piece in the glove compartment of the car seems to work just as well!)

Sailors could carry Elder amulets or trust their well-being to the home-based Elder. All the time their families could see that the tree was alive and well so the sailor would be likewise, but, if the tree sickened or died then that was a very bad omen. Forces beyond the power of the tree were at work.

It is remembered that the Irish (at least) would not include any piece of Elder wood in the construction of a boat. Whether that dates from when the tree came to be feared as dangerously evil or whether it is part of a different belief altogether is not known to the writer.

PROTECTING LIVESTOCK

Being of such economic importance, livestock around a homestead were given equal consideration and any door-ways which they used had Elder duly planted beside them, especially stables and cattle stalls. The trees were expected to ward off all evil, of which the most feared caused loss of weight or death.

In common with the Rowan (*Sorbus aucuparia*), sticks of Elder wood were fashioned into crosses and fixed up inside the stalls to ward off evil, probably illustrating the grafting together of Christianity and the older faiths. The arms of the crosses were usually of equal length. Simple boughs of other plants, such as Hawthorn and Wayfaring Tree and the massive roots of the White Bryony, were also hung up for this purpose.

In particular, Elder was planted around dairy doors and windows to protect the milk. Our ancestors had difficulty explaining why milk 'turned' or 'went off' unless of course the evil spirits had tampered with it. The nearby bushes were convenient for spreading cheese cloths etc. to dry and in so doing they picked up the odour of the leaves. This was deemed to be part of the tree's power which was carried back into the dairy with the cloth - an example of 'sympathetic magic'. To some extent it worked since the odour is fly repellent and so reduces the risk of fly-borne organisms infecting the milk.

PROTECTING BAKEHOUSES

How dangerous to fold the Devil into the bread dough without knowing and then to shove him into a hot oven! Surely all hell will be let loose. As a safeguard the tops of the loaves were split to leave an escape route for the devil and of course we still have split-crust loaves today. Even bread rolls were split and if not, then they were sanctified with the Christian Cross as per the Hot Cross Buns of Good Friday. For a more complete reassurance Elders were grown by the bakehouse door and windows.

In 1989 when the last of the four bakehouses at Cobham, Surrey, was due for demolition the site was visited for drawing and there, all around the main bakehouse were Elder trees. There were none around the outbuildings or by the perimeter fence, so it was unlikely that these had been sown in bird-droppings. They looked as though they had been left there intentionally.

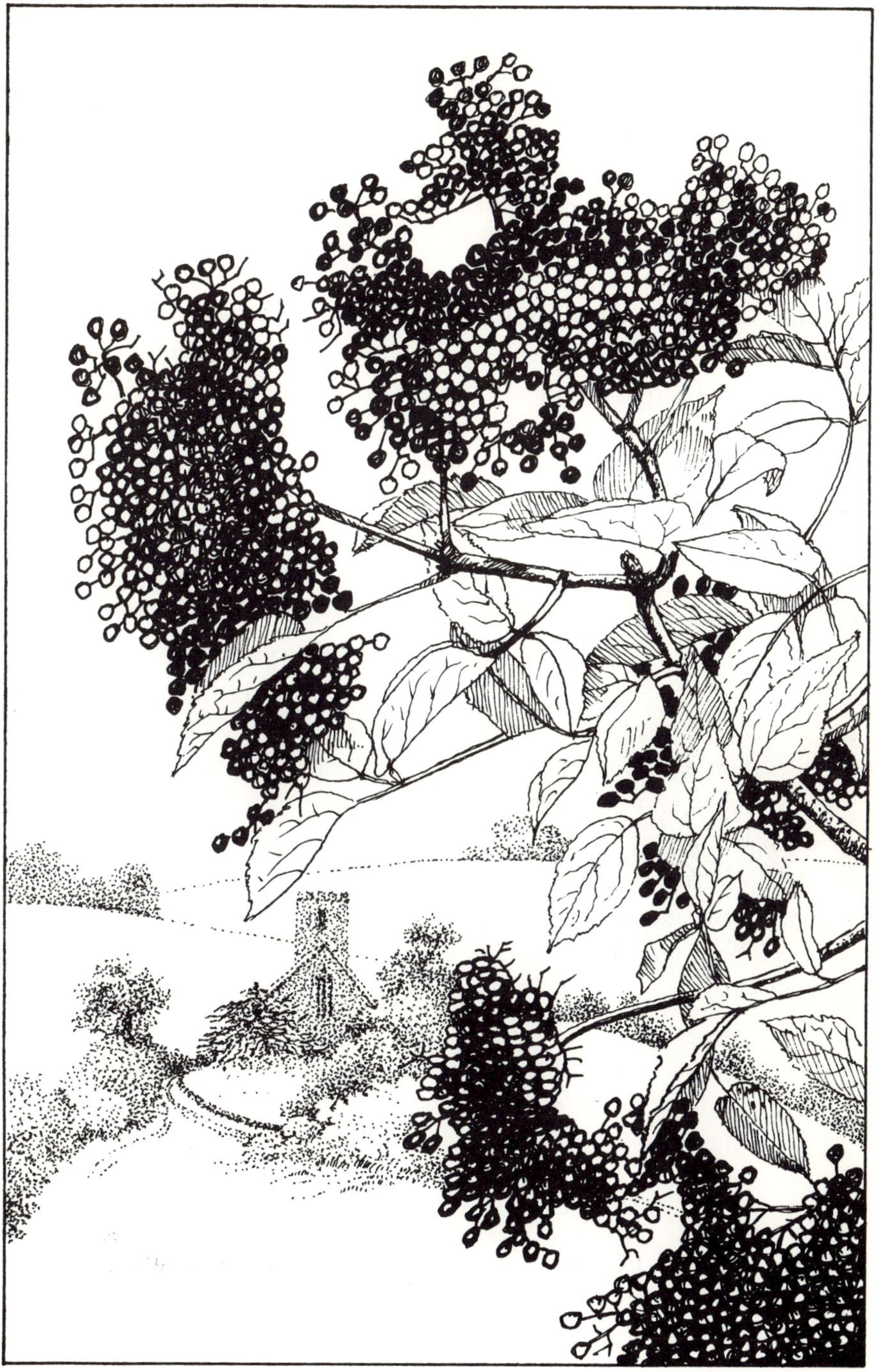

"NEVER CUT THE ELDER TREE"

Cutting Elder is taboo. Not only is that known widely today but it is still practised, or rather, avoided. Now that the tree has been introduced as a Mother Goddess the tradition makes more sense. It does not seem quite right to lop a piece off a goddess does it? In some districts it was possible to cut and take the wood if it was dead, but certainly not the living. In either case it was definitely not to be used as firewood.

The Elder is unique among British trees for having hollow stems and thereby providing ready-made wooden tubes. Additionally it is a very hard wood that takes polish for a good finish. These vitues made it desirable, so there needed to be a way of taking the wood without suffering from a revenge attack. Preliminary rituals ensured safety. Firstly, your reason for needing the wood must be explained, out loud, to the tree/goddess. Then she must be asked, politely, out loud. The correct politeness came to mean approaching the tree quietly but not stealthily, removing one's hat and keeping the arms crossed over the chest to ensure bladed tools will not be brought into use prematurely. For complete humbleness, keep the knees part bent. Wait for Hylde-Moer to give her consent, which she does through silence (sometimes this is interpreted as giving Hylde-Moer time to move out of the way of the blade). Some districts require this ritual to be performed before taking anything - flowers, berries, bark etc. - rather than just the wood.

You don't get anything for nothing, so when asking, you promise to give her back some of your own timber in due course. The words of the most commonly cited request goes something like:

> Mother Elder give me some of thy wood
> And I will give thee some of mine,
> When it's grown enough in the woods.

This may sound a bit like bribery today but in the barter system of pre-monetary days everything was trade in this way and so it would not have sounded anything but normal. Children sent for fruit or flowers were instructed to ask politely and simply:

> Mother Elder, please may I have....

Taking without asking amounts to theft and that was taken extremely seriously in the past. It occurs comparatively rarely in medieval crime records - whatever you had was through the grace of God and therefore to take something of someone else's was to steal God's pleasure. Taking from Mother Elder was also a risk as she was believed to take revenge - you will die within three days.

"NEVER BURN ELDER WOOD"

As with cutting, the burning of Elder does not seem very wise when it was believed to have a potent spiritual content. It is likely that the traditions associated with fire are the oldest of all. The very name 'elder' has devolved from such Saxon words as 'aeld' for fire and 'ellaern' meaning to kindle a fire. The usual explanations for this are that either the pith from inside the stems was gathered and dried for use as kindling material or else that the hollow stems were blown through to kindle the embers. Both make sense but there is a third suggestion - that trapped in the language is a lingering echo of days when it is thought that Elder wood was used in sacred and ritual fires, including funeral pyres.

If Elder wood was indeed burned ritually in honour of the Elder Mother then it could well have been the preserve of the 'priests' which left the uninitiated banned from burning the sacred wood. Another explanation may lie in a fear of attracting death, from its probable connections with funeral rites and with funeral pyres. Perhaps they believed that through death the Elder Mother was reunited with her 'child' and so pieces of the tree, often the living tree, whether green wood or green leaves, were put into graves and coffins. Some think that the Saxons planted it over the graves of executed criminals so that the tree would absorb their evil and purify their souls. Obviously the links were maintained, for as late as 1579 Edmund Spenser was using the funeral connection in the imagery in the *November* poem of his *Shepherd's Calendar*, while in Shakespeare's *Cymbeline* it is a symbol of grief.

Many are the taboos against burning Elder but only recently was the writer told that if Elder is thrown into a fire the 'witch' therein can be heard to scream. Having been brought up in a community afraid to burn any part of the tree, this was news indeed and so, after some deliberation, it was decided to test it.

Yes - the wood does scream - with a loud seering sound! For this a scientific explanation was sought from which it was learned that the Elder is unusual in having air vessels that are twisted, to spiral round the hollow stem, and it was suggested that this sets up tensions in the heat of the fire, which 'scream' as they tear apart. This release of tension can propel globules of boiling sap which could explain the belief that if Elder is thrown in a fire the Devil will spit at you.

Burning it on the household fire will attract the Devil down the chimney. This may be as simple as it sounds or it might be an echo of Norse beliefs connected with Woden who was apparently prone to drop through smoke-holes on a passing visit - the notion adopted in America when 'Father Christmas' was invented. It was Woden who was, in part, celebrated with the great fires of the midwinter festival of Yule.

ELSTEAD, Surey, was spelt Ellenstede in 1128 - the place of the Elder trees, from when the Ellen tree was held in high esteem locally. The pagan beliefs persisted late in S.W.Surrey; to the south is Thursley (honouring Thor), to the north is Tuesley (honouring Tiw of Tuesday fame) and Eashing (named after the Ash trees, sacred as the ancestor of all men and commemorated further north at Esher and Ashford). Nobody knows whether there was ever a sacred grove of Elders at Elstead but the most likely site for one would have been adjacent to the present Christian church site.

THE CONFLICT OF FAITHS

So far, Elder/Hylde-Moer has been in a largely benign light yet much of what is remembered today makes this the most evil of all trees, home of witches and the possession of the Devil. How can this be?

The most likely explanation, and one that applies to many other British plants, is that the Elder was condemned by the Christian Church. When the missionaries began their evangelizing they needed to suppress all the old beliefs which was asking a lot in terms of faith when those old beliefs had given the basic sense of security. England was one of the last great bastions of paganism. Beyond its borders, Ireland, Wales and Scotland were already changing under the influence of the Celtic or Irish Church when Augustine arrived at Canterbury to take on the English, with the Roman version of Christianity. Not everything was vanquished. For example, the use of evergreen plants during the midwinter festival had to be accepted into the new faith, which received the official sanction from Pope Gregory I in AD 604, with a verse in Isaiah to give it authority.

Although much of the old faiths was accepted into Christianity the two did co-exist for hundreds of years. Tree worship was still rife in the 11th century so King Cnut banned it by the law of the land. Even in late Norman times the Norse beliefs were still so well known that they could play a meaningful part in church art even in the far south of England. Hylde-Moer was even more resilient, so that it took until the 14th century for her name to evolve out of Elder Mother. Considering how late that is, makes it all the more surprising that we know so little about her but we can guess with some degree of certainty that the early Christians would have wanted to suppress her, for as a mother goddess she could be a rival to the Blessed Virgin Mary. In maligning the Elder, the Church gave it a role in the worst two events in the life of Christ: the Betrayal and the Crucifixion.

THE BETRAYAL OF JESUS

The Betrayal was brought about by Judas Iscariot taking thirty pieces of silver in return for identifying Jesus to the arresting officers. When he was subsequently condemned to death Judas was overcome with repentance, returned the blood money, and went off to hang himself. So much says the Bible. Legend has added that it was upon an Elder tree that he died. Thus the tree was condemned by association - for aiding a man to commit sin.

This tradition was well-known in England by the 14th century when Langland wrote into *Piers Plowman*:
>Judas he japed with Jewen silver
>And sithen an eller hanged hymselve.

Indeed, in the Holy Land they were showing off the very tree as one of the tourist attractions, according to the 14th century author of the *Travels of Sir John Mandeville*. Hard by the Pool at Shiloam he was shown the
>"Tree of Eldre that Judas henge himself upon, for despeyr
>that he hadde, when he solde and betrayed oure Lord."

The notion persisted; Shakespeare expected his audiences to understand his reference to it in *Loves Labours Lost* and people still know it today. It was perpetuated to some extent through herbal medicine, which utilized the Elder's particular fungus, *Herneola auricula-Judae*, looking like a human ear growing out of the wood. It was deemed to be the ear of Judas and because Judas hanged himself by the throat so the fungus was taken to be good for throat problems. John Gerard in his *Herbal* of 1597 claimed it "taketh away inflammations of the mouth and throat if they be washed therewith,"* and in 1655 Sir Thomas Browne reported it had "become a famous medicine in quinsies, sore throats and strangulation ever since." In 1710 this still found currency in Salmon's *English Herbal*.

*although he preferred to identify *Circis siliquastrum* as the Judas Tree.

ELDER AT THE CRUCIFIXION

The second reason for condemning the Elder was the belief that it provided the timber for Christ's Cross. This was popularised in the *Golden Legend*, the best selling medieval handbook to the Faith, by Jacobus de Voragine. Therein the Elder is described as the Tree of Death, the tree upon which criminals were executed, so its former goodness was well and truly lost.

There's nothing odd about the timber being identified. Religious Houses throughout Christendom claimed to have a piece of the True Cross among their relics and many an 'expert' went on a pilgrimage to view and indentify these. Elder does not feature. In the 8th century The Venerable Bede recorded in his *Collectaneis* that the Cross had been made of Cypress, Cedar, Pine and Box, to which others were soon adding the Palm. John Evelyn in his *Silva* of 1644, cited Lipsius, Falconius, Alphonsus Ciacconius, and Angelus Rocca among these 'learned men' who went off to see for themselves, and the 'old verse':

> Nailed were his Feet to Cedar, to Palm his Hands,
> Cypress his Body bore, Title on Olive stands.

He discounts the lot in favour of Oak, which was commonly used for all manner of purposes whereas the other timbers were too rare and precious for the execution of one deemed a 'malefactor'. Further, he recalls the heaviness of Oak and that Jesus stumbled under the weight of his Cross on the road to Calvary. He thought that the idea of using no less than four timbers must have been based upon old texts 'without any manner of Probability' and concludes,

> 'Let this therefore pass for an errant legend.'

THE CURSE

God was said to have responded to these two associations by cursing the Elder - endowing it with its foul stink as a reminder of the foul deeds of Judas Iscariot. The *Golden Legend* informed readers that it stank from the bodies of criminals executed upon it and from growing among their rotting corpses. Another part of the curse was to wither the large and luscious fruits to little berries, just as the fine stature of this forest tree was reduced to the gnarled and twisted dwarf of today. See how it bows its head in shame; see how the boughs are still bent from the weight of Judas.

> Bour-tree, bour-tree, cookit rung,
> Never straight, and never strong,
> Ever bush, and never tree
> Since our Lord was nailed t'ye.

(Robert Chambers; Popular Rhymes of Scotland; 1847. Bour-tree is Elder)

WITCHES AND FAERIES

Whatever sanctity the Elder might have derived from having borne the body of Christ was soon lost. By the end of the Middle Ages it was largely a tree of superstition, associated with witches (the evil spirits) and faeries (souls not good enough for Heaven nor bad enough for Hell - not the 'fairies' of the later children's books). When the branches of Elder trees by the cottage doors thrashed in the wind it was now said that witches were riding them like steeds.

By the time of the 17th century witch hunts in England the Elder does not surface again as significantly as might be imagined. On the whole it seems to have been safe to have an Elder outside the door without being suspected of witchcraft, whereas some of the other plants were decidedly suspect, like Thornapple, *Datura stramonium*, which was put into 'flying ointments' for witches to rub into their thighs whenever they were to take flight. By that time the notions of witches were changing. Now they were becoming real people - your family and neighbours, as the witch hunts purged village after village. Lesser, unseen, forces became the faeries, referred to as witches whenever it was necessary to emphasise seriousness.

Sacred groves became places of faerie and the woodland spirits were said to favour clumps of Elders. Wherever two thorns and an Elder grew together was a very special place, to be treated with respect. The woodland spirits, like all the 'Little Folk', love music and merrymaking. They respond most favourably to music from instruments made of elderwood which comes ready hollow, just needing the bore polishing up - hence names like Bour Tree, Boon Tree, Bore Tree, Borral, Boun Tree, Bountry and Pipe Tree. In the 1st century AD Pliny recorded it being used for the shrillest pipes and the most sonorous horns providing the wood was culled from beyond the sound of the crowing cocks. Fifes, trumpets, flutes, penny-whistles and the chanters of bagpipes have all been so made. On such lists there is usually an ancient Greek instrument called a sambuke after which Linnaeus named the genus Sambucus but whatever the ancient writers were referring to has been lost. It was not the sambuck of the Romans as so often thought as this was a triangular stringed instrument! Neither did the sackbut derive from it, for although this is a wind instrument, it's name derives from an Old French verb meaning to pull, because it had a slide like a trombone.

MAY EVE

April 30th, the Eve of May Day, was one of the days in the calendar when evil forces were most feared of being particularly active. The Elder was one of the plants that featured in the May Day celebrations and as the May Bough in Ireland. This great time in the annual social calendar was not to be spoiled by evil forces, so we read that "in order to prevent witches from entering their houses, the common people used to gather Elder leaves on the last day of April and affix them to their doors and windows."

(William Coles, The Art of Simpling, 1656).

Interestingly, Coles puts this in the past tense but in some districts the practice persisted until recent times. It is certainly old and was apparently widespread. Certainly it was known to the later Saxons from their German homeland where it was called Walpurgis Night.

Walpurgis (probably from Walburga) was an 8th century English nun who became a Christian missionary and finally an abbess. She gave her name to this date because it was the day when her remains were moved from Heidenheim to Eichstatt. There, oil which was claimed to have healing properties, seeped out of the rocks and thus the place became an important centre of pilgrimage for the sick and where many of the old pagan cures must have been kept alive. That applied to England too, for in 1655 Sir Thomas Browne observed "The common people keep as a good secret in curing wounds the leaves of the Elder, which they have gathered the last day of April." This became an important medicine as 'Green Elder Ointment' or 'Unguentum Sambuci Viride'. Likewise, the oil of Elder leaves, known as 'Green Oil' or 'Oil of Swallows' came to be used as a liniment. It was made by soaking crushed leaves in linseed or rape oil.

May 1st is sometimes listed as the Feast Day of Walpurgis but
that fell officially on February 25th, the day of her death in AD 779.

MIDSUMMER AND ST JOHN

Caution is needed over references to Midsummer as so many modern notions have been backdated on to it. Once it had been an important festival, heralding a new season, which the early missionaries failed to suppress. So they superimposed on it the Feast of St. John the Baptist because he heralded the coming of Christ. During this process some of the events of the heathen year got transposed and so the fire rituals for St. John's Eve (June 23rd) came from the Lammas celebrations, due later in the year. Significant plants, which came to be known as the 'Herbs of St. John', were gathered for ritual use and these included the Elder blossom. All the herbs were tied in bunches, attached to sticks and dangled over one of the sacred fires. These were not beacon fires but smokey ones to produce 'holy smoke' to drive out evil to make room for God's blessing. Once the herbs had been smoked (cured, like bacon up a chimney) they would last in this preserved state until the ritual was repeated the following year. They were safeguarded as protective amulets, especially for all aspects of dairying. They were hung up in cow stalls and the dairy to ward off all evil influences.

Midsummer is of course one of the great faery days in the year, much popularised by the writers of children's fairy tale books. All round Britain, and on the Continent, it is believed widely that being in the company of an Elder tree at this time will ensure that you see the Fairy King and his retinue ride by. The early literature ensures we do not miss this colourful event, whether in the Seelie Court of Scotland or with Ireland's Daoine Sidhe, (pronounced Theena She), or wherever.

EPIPHANY

The end of the year is one of the prime times for fear of evil forces at work, such as Hallowe'en on October 31st and Twelth Night on January 6th. Then, it was feared, the forces would have their final fling.

Twelth Night had to be accepted into the Christian calendar and so this became Epiphany - the day when the Church remembered the infant Christ being shown to the Magi (representing the Gentiles). The word epiphany is ancient Greek meaning to show or to makemanifest. It was important that nothing less than holy should make its presence felt and so towards this end there was a ritual that involved Elder berries. They were placed in a circle on the ground and in this ring stood the fearful seeking protection. This practice seems to have survived longest in parts of Germany and Austria where this is 'Bertha Night' - Bertha being a personification of the notion of Epiphany and appears as a pale lady in nurseries to rock the baby gently to sleep. Some of the informants relating their memories of this thought it was an act of compassion in compensation for their being no mother to comfort the baby. Behave badly, however, and Bertha would teach children the error of their ways, just as the Elder Mother was believed to do. By the 19th century children were being told that she'd had massive feet and a great iron nose.

The Italian version of this features not Bertha but Befana who was the good fairy who delivered the children's Christmas presents. This aspect is much the same as that for St. Nicholas or Father Christmas in the rituals of other cultures. Someone, acting as Befana had to creep stealthily into the children's room on Twelve Night to leave the presents.

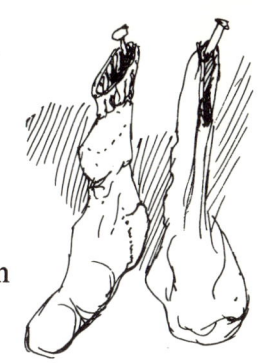

Of course, to be able to safeguard these proceedings with Elder berries means they must be dried ones, gathered the previous year in readiness for this need. Now for the snag. They *must* have been gathered upon St.John's Night. That being June 24th means it is an impossibility because the tree is in blossom, not fruit, at that date. This is one of a number of impossible pieces of folklore gathered and this impossibilty seems to be significant. For instance, St.John's is the time to collect fern seed (Bracken being the fern in question) and everyone wanted fern seed because that had the power to make you invisible! H.G.Wells was not the first person for whom this had appeal!

Sadly, ferns never flower to make seeds. Even the spores are not ready at this time, so it's no good going out with your Hazel stick to tap the seeds on to the black leather binding of your Bible whatever the lore says. That is not quite true. You CAN get the fern seed. For the power to do it, you need simply to perform the magic circle ritual with the Elder berries at Epiphany!

NARCOTIC VISIONS

Seeing the Fairy King and his retinue ride by may not be as fanciful at it seems at first. There are so many references to having visions and odd experiences under Elder trees that it is now wondered whether the strong odour of the foliage contains narcotic compounds which induce some sort of hallucinations in susceptible people, (as per Yew trees). As early as 1776 one of the foremost doctors in the land, William Withering, observed:

> "The whole plant hath a narcotic smell;
> it is not well to sleep under its shade."

People warned that you would never wake up if you slept under an Elder tree.

Whether or not modern science will justify these fears, the tree is known already for having powerful compounds. It will yield powerful emetics and purges for herbal medicine. It exudes some sort of growth retarder to suppress competitive growth so that the ground under an Elder is invariably bare of other plants. Its pungent foliage is fly repellent and has even been claimed to repel mice (although this does not work with the field mice that come into my garage in the winter!)

The insecticidal qualities have been used for centuries, even on a commercial basis in that the market gardens around London in the first half of the 19th century tried growing the tree in large numbers to protect the crops from insect attack. "Extravagent plantations" of them existed there as early as the 17th century according to Evelyn. Anyone thinking of trying this on the home plot should bear in mind that growing Elders next to vegetables was said to extinguish the male line in the family.

Beware of following the old practice of rubbing the leaves into the skin for insect repellent purposes, as the skin of some people

Although the leaves do deter flies (as opposed to fleas, lice, ants etc.) and have been made into insecticidal sprays, horticultural soaps etc. they are only effective against certain species. Many small flies can be seen on the blossoms and these are in part responsible for pollination, (although the tree is largely self-pollinating). For the same service sprays of Elder have been worn in hats or in the bridles of horses.

Dairy doors and windows had Elders planted beside them, to ward off evil that would 'turn' the milk. Consequently they were placed conveniently for following the traditional decree that all cheese cloths, and other cloths used in dairying, should be spread over an Elder bush to dry. It was said that these cloths then absorbed the tree's magic powers and carried them back into the dairy to continue as a protective force. This sounds like a practical exploitation of the narcotic compounds.

The smell of the blossom has also become part of folklore:

> Hawthorn blooms and Elderflowers
> Fill the house with evil powers.

Both these flowers were condemned by Puritans and Victorians alike, for smelling of sex or sin, while the Elderflowers smell of death to some people. They are just two of over seventy flowers which are 'unlucky' to bring indoors.

MAGIC HEALING

Folk beliefs did not stop the Puritan minds of the 17th century from exploring the values of the tree, especially for medicines. It was then that the Apothecaries were vying with the Surgeons for independent recognition and one of the former, Nicholas Culpeper, affronted the Surgeons by translating their medical knowledge from Latin into English for all the literate world to use. He found much to recommend the Elder and other writers could compile a whole treatise on the tree: one ran to over 200 pages, covering over 70 human ailments. Evelyn observed:

> "If the Medicinal Properties of the Leaves, Bark, Berries, etc. were thoroughly known, I cannot tell what our country-man could ail, for which he might not fetch a Remedy from every Hedge, either for sickness or wound."
> (Silva; Bk 1; Ch.XX. 18)

Obviously such knowledge was not universal yet was known well enough for Shakespeare to risk losing the point when he hailed it with two of the other great medical authorities:

> "What says my Æsculapius? My Galen? My heart of Elder?"
> (Merry Wives of Windsor; Act II; Sc.3)

Similarly, Ettmeuller called it "the medicine chest of the country people" and there is also the much-quoted reference to the Dutch physician Boerhaave raising his hat in reverence to any Elder he passed. Perhaps this was a widespread gesture as a lady at a talk in 1994 reported her husband doing this to Hawthorn trees; part of the folklore he'd brought with him from Ireland. From North America came a reference (source not traced) that the Norse goddess Freyja took up residence in an Elder for "its beneficial medicinal qualities." As she was a fertility goddess, maybe this, association is valid.

Although Evelyn saw the tree as a valuable cure-all, he condemned the smell of it, associating it with disease. In that he was not far wrong in that Elders grow beside muck-heaps, open drains and other unhealthy places. Less probable are some of the other notions. For example, it was said that making compacts of soil from beneath Elder trees could be used successfully for relieving toothache. It was said also that the tree would attract tuberculosis to the house. Very popular however, were Elder amulets carried on the person to ward off such afflictions as St. Anthony's Fire, rheumatism and epilepsy. This protectionism or sympathetic magic makes people smile today - yet these are often the same people who wear a lucky St. Christopher or a crucifix, have a rabbit's foot on their key-ring or take a lucky mascot into exams!

More prevalent was the 'cure' for warts (the mark of the Devil) which exploited the notion of 'transference' and could involve any one from a wide range of plants. Particular parts of the plant were rubbed onto the warts in the belief that the 'evil' would be transferred to the plant. The potato became the most frequently recommended plant to be so used. After rubbing the 'evil' off onto it, the root was to be taken away and buried. Suitable sites for burial were beside routeways, preferrably busy ones such as crossroads, where a passer-by could 'catch' the evil and take it away with them. All manner of chants and spells accompanied this ritual and varied from district to district. In 1996 a member of an audience produced from his pocket what looked like a small brown pebble that made a pebble-like noise on the table. It was, however a dried potato which he had carried with him many a long year since he had broken his ankles and been told that although they had mended he could expect chronic rheumatism in later life. So far that prognosis has not been fulfilled, and so with a smile he put the potato back in his pocket.

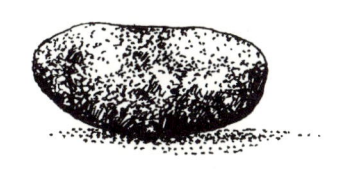

EVERYDAY LIFE

CRADLES

"Never build Elder wood into a cradle" asserts the old lore. If you do, then the baby will sicken and die. Alternatively, it will attract the Devil will be attracted down the chimney to sleep on baby's face and suffocate it, or it will attract witches who will pinch the baby black and blue all over until it dies. These all sound like 'cot deaths' today. Nothing has changed. We simply look in different directions for explanations. More ominous is the warning that the Devil will come and steal the child, or, that Hylde-Moer will come out of the wood and torment the baby mercilessly until it is removed from the cradle - what an odd thing for the Elder Mother to do. Perhaps these are all later ideas from Christians intent upon stamping out lingering loyalties to trees that had once been sacred. Remnants of the rituals were decried as 'superstitions'.

STRIKING

Striking with Elder sticks conveys evil into the subject. Goads or gads for animals had to be of another wood (usually the Rowan, *Sorbus aucuparia*) unless gall flies were active. These insects are troublesome in their season for stinging the legs and undersides of cattle which made them difficult to control. This was dangerous in the days when cattle still had horns, and long horns at that. On these occasions it was decreed that the Elder had to be cut through the leaf joints (nodes) so as not to open the hollow centre and let evil out. Why there should be evil in there at all is not remembered by the people spoken to today. Indeed, why Elder should be chosen at all is not clear. Perhaps it is an extension of its insecticidal qualities but it doesn't sound very likely.

Even more peculiar is the injunction from Christopher Gullet in 1772 (*Philosophical Transactions*) to whip turnips, cabbages, corn and fruit trees with Elder twigs to ward off blight. Certainly wilting vegetation has little attraction to sap-sucking insects! Maybe this is a very ancient relic from the Celtic rituals. Apparently the Celts had no 'harvest festival' to give thanks to the fertility deities because they expected a harvest since they had performed the necessary fertility rituals at the beginning of the season. With this in mind, the Elder twig flogging has a hint of sense about it.

None of this explains why children should not be struck with Elder sticks unless again it's fear of conveying evil, as per livestock. Disobey this taboo and it was said the child would stop growing, but, that would be desirable in times when being small was considered beautiful. Babies were rubbed with an ointment made from Daisies *(Bellis perennis)* to stunt their growth. It didn't work. The plant has been investigated, in vain, for a growth retarder (which might have been valuable in cancer treatments). In places where this taboo on striking with Elder sticks covered all ages then the hand of the victim was said to come out of the grave for you.

COOKING AND WATER

'Never use Elder wood to make a meat skewer for poultry' is still known widely. However, skewers were an important use for the very hard wood of this tree. Perhaps they were reserved for red meats whereas the blander white meats of poultry could pick up the strong unpleasant taste of the Elder. Goose meat would be an exception since it is as dark and as strong tasting as beef.

Similarly, "Never let Elder roots grow into the well water," suggests that taste is imparted. Nevertheless, at least five holy wells in Ireland are associated with Elders (so the Christian Church has not outlawed Elder completely). Indeed, the tree was encouraged around surface water, such as drinking troughs and water buts, perhaps for its fly repellent properties.

INDEX OF OTHER PLANTS

Ash 16
Box 19
Bracken 25
Cedar 19
Cypress 19
Elder, American 5
  Black 5
  Dog 55
  Dutch 5
  European 5
  Ground 5
  Red-berried 5

Hawthorn 8, 27-8
Hazel 25
Jews Ear fungus 18
Oak 19
Palm 19
Pine 19
Rowan 8, 30
Thornapple 20
Wayfaring Tree 8
White Bryony 8
Yew 26

INDEX OF MAIN THEMES

Bake houses 10
Befana 25
Betrayal 18
Boats 8
Botanical 5
Bread 10
Bertha Night 24
Burning 14-15
Christianity 17
Cradels 30
Cruicifiction 17
Cutting 12-13
Dairy 27
Daoine Sidhe 23
Epiphany 24
Fire 14
Food 31
Funerals 14
Fern-seed 25
Good Friday 10
Homes 6-7
Hylde Moer 6
Hilde Vinde 6

Insecticide 26-7
Judes 18-19
Land 7
Livestock 8-9
Lightning 7
May 22
Medicine 28-29
Mid-summer 23
Milk 9, 23
Mother goddess 6
Music 21
Norse 15-16, 28
Punishment 30
Travellers 8
Sailors 8
Seelie Court 23
St. Johns 23, 25
Thor 15
Walpurgis 22
Water 31
Witches 20-21
Wood 12